First published in 1981 by
Usborne Publishing Ltd,
83-85 Saffron Hill,
London EC1N 8RT, England.

© Usborne Publishing Ltd 1988, 1981

The name Usborne and the device are
Trade Marks of Usborne Publishing Ltd.

About this book

This lively book of animals is designed to amuse as well as instruct. Children of all ages are fascinated by the world of animals and they will return to this delightful reference book again and again.

Very young children will enjoy looking at and talking about the amusing illustrations. With the help of an adult, they can be encouraged to identify the animals and read their names.

Older children will find this book helpful and stimulating when they begin to write their own stories and poems. From the pictures, they will be able to learn how and where particular animals live. Unfamiliar, as well as familiar, animals have been included in order to extend children's knowledge of the animal kingdom.

The complete index of all words at the back of the book will encourage children to look up words in alphabetical order. This is most useful when starting to use dictionaries and encyclopedias.

This book provides a wide range of opportunities to read words, spell words and use words. It is an exciting journey into the world of animals.

Betty Root

**Centre for the Teaching of Reading
University of Reading**

Can you find the frog ?

On every picture across two pages there is a frog to look for. Can you find it ?

THE
ANIMAL
Picture Word Book

Claudia Zeff

Illustrated by Nick Price

Consultant: Betty Root

By the pond

water vole

snail

reeds

kingfisher

otter

frog

water lily

pond weed

newt

swan

maggots

minnows

swallow

frog's eggs

tadpoles

4

net

harvest mouse

grebe

water shrew

heron

wren

pike

stickleback   grasshopper   dragonfly   ducklings   duck

5

On the seashore

gull

tern

plover

oyster-catcher

seaweed

barnacles

periwinkles

pebbles

blenny

sand eel

sea anemone

sea urchin

starfish

oyster

limpets

6

curlew

cormorant

lobster

razor shell

crab

cockles

mussels

egg case   octopus   whelks   scallop   cuttlebone   prawn

chipmunk

moose

wolf

elk

raccoon

porcupine

black bear

8

In the mountains

beaver

mink

skunk

red fox

cave

mountain goat

grizzly bear

puma

salmon

quail

maple tree

berries

marmot

woodchuck

bighorn sheep

pine cones

eagle

wild turkey

9

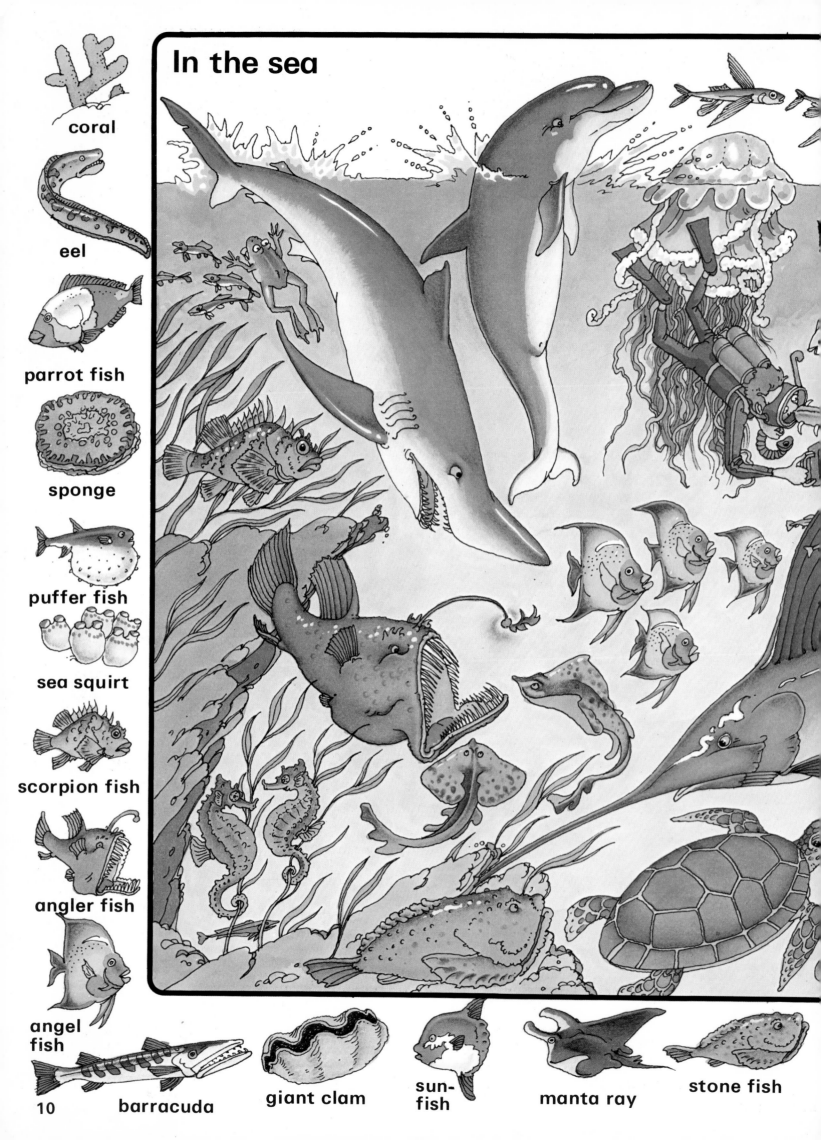

In the sea

coral

eel

parrot fish

sponge

puffer fish

sea squirt

scorpion fish

angler fish

angel fish

10 barracuda

giant clam

sun-fish

manta ray

stone fish

dolphin

shark

skate

swordfish

turtle

flying fish

jellyfish

sea horse   sawfish   cuttlefish   aqualung   diver

At the waterhole

hippo potamus

python

elephant

zebra

bustard

termites' nest

water buffalo

lion cub

12 lion

gnu

lioness

hyena

flamingo

gazelle

crane

giant anteater

nest

weaver bird

baobab tree

pelican

warthog

giraffe

rhinoceros

jackal

baboon

cheetah

acacia tree

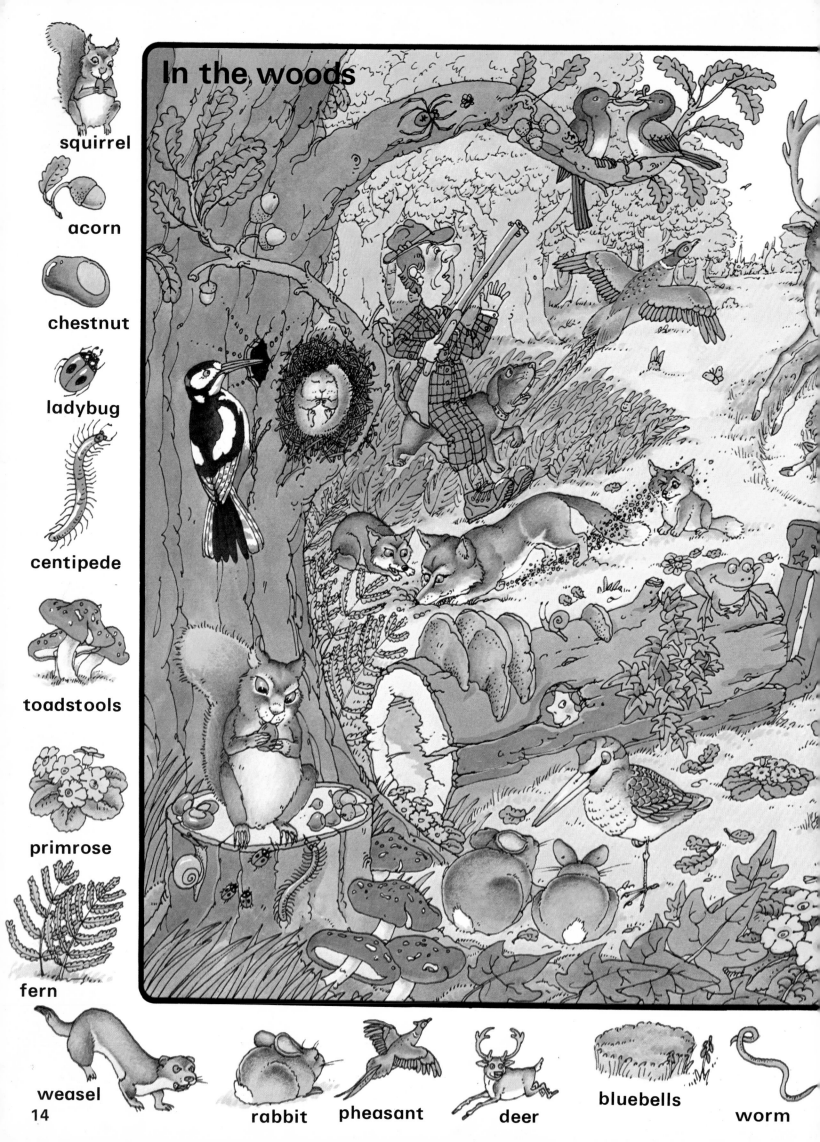

In the woods

squirrel

acorn

chestnut

ladybug

centipede

toadstools

primrose

fern

weasel

14

rabbit

pheasant

deer

bluebells

worm

dormouse

woodpecker

butterfly

mistletoe

mole

molehill

woodcock

oak tree

crow

robin

fox

badger

15

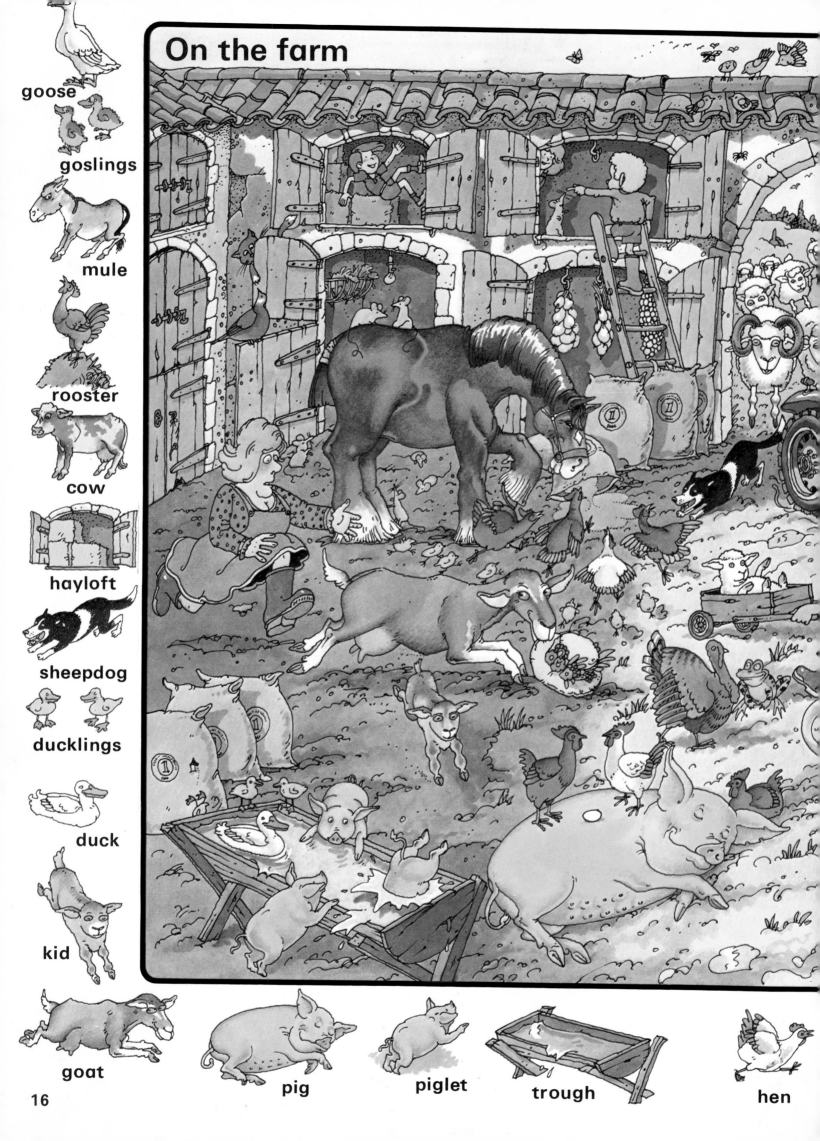

On the farm

goose

goslings

mule

rooster

cow

hayloft

sheepdog

ducklings

duck

kid

goat

pig

piglet

trough

hen

16

bull

turkey

tractor

ram

lamb

sheep

bales of hay

chicks

cat

work horse

cowshed

sack of corn

stable

Deserts

date palm

prickly pear cactus

cactus

jack rabbit

oasis

vulture

beetle

tarantula

dromedary

camel

kangaroo rat

scorpion

rattlesnake

toad

18

ostrich

ostrich egg

fennec fox

hawk

owl

nomad

bobcat

foal

donkey

addax

oryx

In the jungle

banana tree

cocoa tree

armadillo

spider monkey

boa constrictor

okapi

jaguar

gorilla

20 opossum

lemur

chimpanzee

fruit bat

pineapple plant

egret

scarlet ibis

creeper

gibbon

orang utan

hummingbird

sloth

toucan

bird of
paradise

parrot

crocodile

spoonbill

iguana

loris

bamboo

21

In frozen lands

seal

seal pup

arctic fox

albatross

puffin

reindeer

musk ox

whale

walrus

ermine

ptarmigan

iceberg

22

snowy owl

polar bear

lemmings

tern

husky dog

penguin

penguin chick

igloo

kayak

sled

spear

Eskimo

23

In Australia

tiger snake

frilled lizard

dingo

finch

joey

kangaroo

emu

emu eggs

wombat

emu chick

koala bear

cub

lyrebird

parakeet

24

wallaby

echidna

rabbit

gum tree

aborigine

eucalyptus
tree

boomerang

cockatoo

stick
insect

kookaburra

bandicoot

platypus

25

At the dog show

greyhound

Pekingese

beagle

Irish setter

dachshund

Scottish terrier

St Bernard

Dobermann pinscher

26 bulldog

boxer

Labrador retriever

poodle

Dalmatian

hare

borzoi

cocker spaniel

Old English sheepdog

corgi

Afghan hound

Great Dane

pug

whippet

bloodhound

Pyrenean mountain dog

German shepherd

chow

basset hound

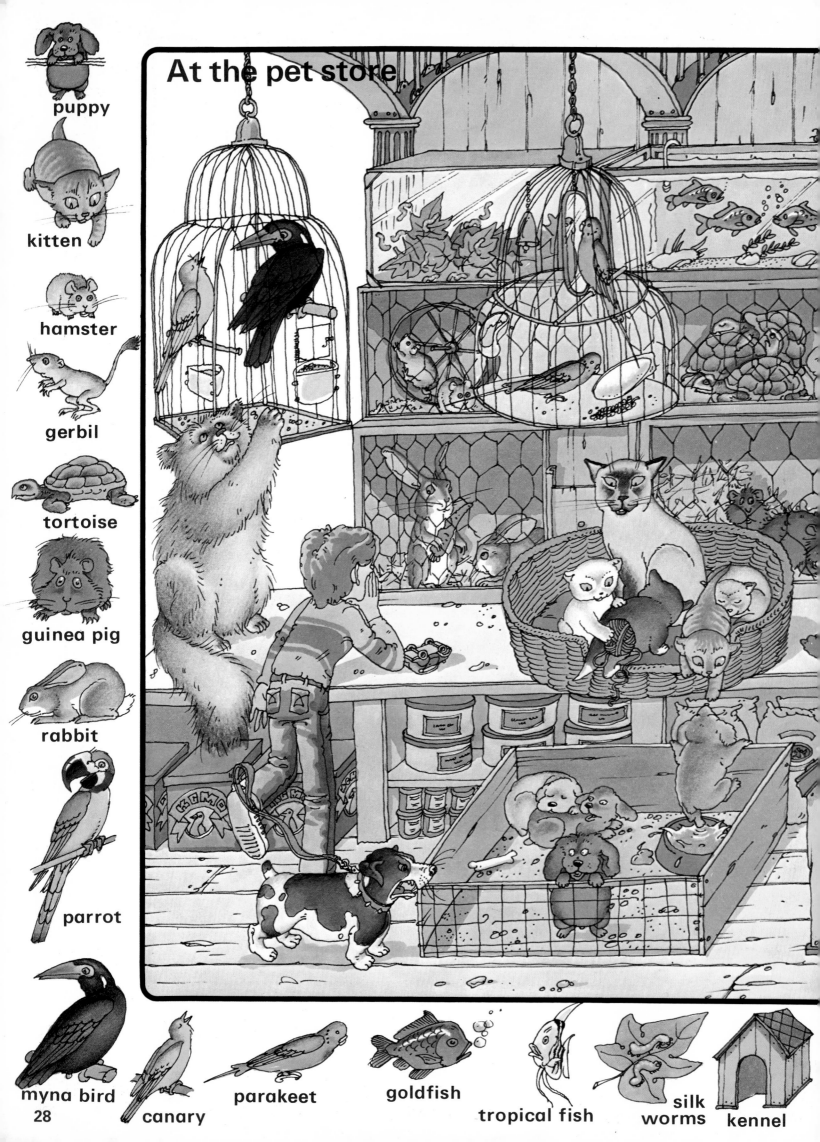

At the pet store

puppy

kitten

hamster

gerbil

tortoise

guinea pig

rabbit

parrot

myna bird

canary

parakeet

goldfish

tropical fish

silk worms

kennel

28

aquarium

birdcage

perch

dog biscuits

leash

collar

straw

basket

blue
Persian
cat

Siamese
cat

monkey

doves

fish bowl

In the town

blue tit

mice

rat

caterpillar

cat

dog

flies

gull

ants

slug

beetle

spider

spider's web

butterfly

moth

30

starling

house martin

hedgehog

rabbit

squirrel

sparrow

wasps

wasps' nest

blackbird

magpie

worms

pigeon

owl

Animal families

stallion (father)

foal

mare (mother)

buck (father)

baby rabbit

doe (mother)

ewe (mother)

lamb

ram (father)

hen (mother)

rooster (father)

chick

drake (father)

duck (mother)

duckling

billy (father)

kid

nanny (mother)

sow (mother)

piglet

boar (father)

buck
(father)

doe
(mother)

fawn

peacock
(father)

chick

peahen (mother)

fox (father)

vixen
(mother)

fox cub

bull
(father)

cow (mother)

calf

dog
(father)

tom
(father)

cat
(mother)

kitten

bitch
(mother)

puppy

goose
(mother)

gosling

gander (father)

cob (father)

pen (mother)

cygnet

33

Animal words

tail

hump

beak

tongue

antlers

trunk

claws

tusk

mane

webbed foot

horns

fleece

quills

hoof

wing

whiskers

teeth

talons

ear

neck

pouch

leg

snout

fin

shell

paw

eye

feathers

scales

fur

Animal homes

rabbits' burrow

storks' nest

anthill

beehive

bears' den

flamingo's nest

squirrel's nest

eagles' eyrie

beavers' lodge

Animal groups

skein of ducks

pride of lions

pack of hounds

school of whales

flight of birds

swarm of locusts

herd of cows

flock of sheep

gaggle of geese

shoal of mackerel

Story book animals

phoenix

demon

winged horse

sea monster

roc

unicorn

mermaid

dragon

centaur

Nighttime animals

bat

mongoose

fireflies

kiwi

hyena

moth

rat

bush baby

owl

badger

cricket

mouse

pangolin

loris

Animals of long ago

dodo

woolly mammoth

quagga

cave bear

Tasmanian wolf

woolly rhinoceros

moa

sabre toothed cat

giant sloth

Dinosaurs

kentrosaurus

tyrannosaurus rex

spinosaurus

anatosaurus

paleoscincus

pteranodon

stegosaurus

triceratops

plesiosaurus

diplodocus

iguanodon

Words in order

This is a list of all the words in the pictures. They are in the same order as the alphabet. After each word is a number. On that page you will find the word and a picture.

a

b

42

black bear, 8
blackbird, 31
blenny fish, 6
bloodhound, 27
blue Persian cat, 29
blue tit, 30
bluebell, 14
boa constrictor, 20
boar (pig), 32
bobcat, 19
boomerang, 25
borzoi, 27
boxer dog, 26
buck (deer), 33
buck (rabbit), 32
buffalo, water, 12
bull, 17, 33
bulldog, 26
burrow (rabbits'), 36
bush baby, 39
bustard, 12
butterfly, 15, 30
by the pond, 4 and 5

C

cactus, 18
cactus, prickly pear, 18
calf, 33
camel, 18
canary, 28
cat, 17, 30, 33
cat (tom), 33
cat basket, 29
cat, blue Persian, 29
cat, sabre-toothed, 40
cat, Siamese, 29
caterpillar, 30
cave, 8
cave bear, 40
centaur, 38
centipede, 14
cheetah, 13
chestnut, 14
chick, 17, 32
chick, emu, 24
chick, peacock, 33
chick, penguin, 23
chimpanzee, 20

chipmunk, 8
chow 27
clam, giant, 10
claw, 34
cob (swan), 33
cockatoo, 25
cocker spaniel, 27
cockle, 7
cocoa tree, 20
collar, 29
coral, 10
corgi, 27
cormorant, 7
corn, sack of, 17
cow, 16, 33
cows, herd of, 37
cowshed, 17
crab, 7
crane, 13
creeper, 21
cricket, 39
crocodile, 21
crow, 15
cub, fox, 33
cub, koala bear, 24
cub, lion, 12
curlew, 7
cuttlebone, 7
cuttlefish, 11
cygnet (swan), 33

d

dachshund, 26
Dalmatian dog, 26
date palm, 18
deer, 14
deer (buck), 33
deer (doe), 33
deer (fawn), 33
demon, 38
den, bears', 36
deserts, 18 and 19
dingo, 24
dinosaurs, 41

diplodocus, 41
diver, 11
Dobermann pinscher, 26
dodo, 40
doe (deer), 33
doe, (rabbit), 32
dog, 30, 33
dog (bitch), 33
dog (puppy), 33
dogs:
    Afghan hound, 27
    basset hound, 27
    beagle, 26
    bloodhound, 27
    borzoi, 27
    boxer, 26
    bulldog, 26
    chow 27
    cocker spaniel, 27
    corgi, 27
    dachshund, 26
    Dalmatian, 26
    Dobermann pinscher, 26
    German shepherd, 27
    Great Dane, 27
    greyhound, 26
    husky, 23
    Irish setter, 26
    Labrador retriever, 26
    Old English sheepdog, 27
    Pekingese, 26
    poodle, 26
    pug, 27
    Pyrenean mountain dog, 27
    St Bernard, 26
    Scottish terrier, 26
    sheepdog, 16
    whippet, 27
dog biscuit, 29
dog show, 26 and 27
dolphin, 11
donkey, 19
dormouse, 15
dove, 29
dragon, 38
dragonfly, 5
drake (duck), 32
drey (squirrel's), 36
dromedary, 18
duck, 5, 16, 32
duck (drake), 32
duckling, 5, 16, 32
ducks, skein of, 37

e

eagle, 9
eagles' eyrie, 36
ear, 35
echidna, 25
eel, 10
eel, sand, 6
egg case, 7
egg, emu, 24
egg, ostrich, 19
egret, 20
elephant, 12
elk, 8
emu, 24
emu chick, 24
emu egg, 24
ermine, 22
Eskimo, 23
eucalyptus tree, 25
ewe (sheep), 32
eye, 35
eyrie (eagles'), 36

f

feather, 35
fennec fox, 19
fern, 14
fin, 35
finch, 24
firefly, 39
fish:

    angel fish, 10
    angler fish, 10
    barracuda, 10
    blenny, 6
    cuttlefish, 11
    eel, 10
    flying fish, 11
    goldfish, 28
    jellyfish, 11

    mackerel, 37
    manta ray, 10
    minnow, 4
    parrot fish, 10
    pike, 5
    puffer fish, 10
    salmon, 9
    sand eel, 6
    sawfish, 11
    scorpion fish, 10
    shark, 11
    skate, 11
    starfish, 6
    stickleback, 5
    stonefish, 10
    sunfish, 10
    swordfish, 11
    tropical fish, 28
fish bowl, 29
flamingo, 12
flamingos' nest, 36
fleece, 34
flies, 30
flight of birds, 37
flock of sheep, 37
flying fish, 11
foal (donkey), 19
foal (horse), 32
fox, 15, 33
fox (vixen), 33
fox cub, 33
fox, arctic, 22
fox, fennec, 19
fox, red, 8
frilled lizard, 24
frog, 4
frog's eggs, 4
fruit bat, 20
fur, 35

g

gaggle of geese, 37
gazelle, 13
gerbil, 28
German shepherd, 27
giant anteater, 13
giant clam, 10

giant sloth, 40
gibbon, 21
giraffe, 13
gnu, 12
goat, 16, 32
goat (kid), 16, 32
goat, billy, 32
goat, mountain, 9
goat, nanny, 32
goldfish, 28
goose, 16, 33
goose (gander), 33
goose (gosling), 16, 33
gorilla, 20
grasshopper, 5
Great Dane, 27
grebe, 5
greyhound, 26
grizzly bear, 9
guinea pig, 28
gull, 6, 30
gum tree, 25

h

hamster, 28
hare, 26
harvest mouse, 5
hawk, 19
hay loft, 16
hay, bales of, 17
hedgehog, 31
hen, 16, 32
herd of cows, 37
heron, 5
hippopotamus, 12
hoof, 34
horn, 34
horse (foal), 32
horse (mare), 32
horse (stallion), 32
horse, winged, 38
horse, sea, 11
hounds, pack of, 37
house martin, 31
hummingbird, 21
hump, 34
husky dog, 23
hyena, 12, 39

i

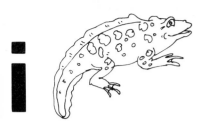

j

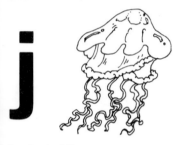

k

l

m

n

o

owl, snowy, 23
oyster, 6
oystercatcher, 6
ox, musk, 22

p

pack of hounds, 37
paleoscincus, 41
palm, date, 18
pangolin, 39
parakeet, 24, 28
parrot, 21, 28
parrot fish, 10
paw, 35
peacock, 33
peacock chick, 33
peahen, 33
pebble, 6
Pekingese, 26
pelican, 13
pen (swan), 33
penguin, 23
penguin chick, 23
perch (bird's), 29
periwinkle, 6
pheasant, 14
phoenix, 38
pig, 16
pig (boar), 32
pig (sow), 32
pig, guinea, 28
pigeon, 31
piglet, 16, 32
pike, 5
pine cone, 9
pineapple plant, 20
platypus, 25
plesiosaurus, 41
plover, 6
polar bear, 23
pond weed, 4,
poodle, 26
porcupine, 8
pouch (kangaroo), 35
prawn, 7

prickly pear cactus, 18
pride of lions, 37
primrose, 14
ptarmigan, 22
pteranodon, 41
puffer fish, 10
puffin, 22
pug dog, 27
puma, 9
pup, seal, 22
puppy, 28, 33
Pyrenean mountain dog, 27
python, 12

q

quagga, 40
quail, 9
quills, 34

r

rabbit, 14, 25, 32
rabbit, (baby), 32
rabbit (buck), 32
rabbit (doe), 32
rabbits' burrow, 36
raccoon, 8
ram (sheep), 17, 32
rat, 30
rat, kangaroo, 18
rattlesnake, 18
razor clam, 7
red fox, 8
reeds, 4
reindeer, 22
rhinoceros, 13
rhinoceros, woolly, 40
robin, 15
roc, 38
rooster, 16, 32

s

sabre toothed cat, 40
sack of corn, 17
St Bernard dog, 26
salmon, 9
sand eel, 6
sawfish, 11
scales (fish), 35
scallop, 7
scarlet ibis, 20
school of whales, 37
scorpion, 18
scorpion fish, 10
Scottish terrier, 26
sea anemone, 6
sea horse, 10
sea monster, 38
sea squirt, 10
sea urchin, 6
seal, 22
seal pup, 22
seaweed, 6
shark, 11
sheep, 17
sheep (ewe), 32
sheep (lamb), 17, 32
sheep (ram), 17, 32
sheep, bighorn, 9
sheep, flock of, 37
sheepdog, 16
shell, razor, 7
shell (snail's), 35
shoal of mackerel, 37
Siamese cat, 29
silk worm, 28
skate, 11
skein of ducks, 37
skunk, 8
sled, 23
sloth, 21
sloth, giant, 40
slug, 30
snail, 4
snake (boa constrictor), 20
snake (python), 12
snake (rattlesnake), 18

snake, tiger, 24
snout, 35
snowy owl, 23
sow (pig), 32
sparrow, 31
spear, 23
spider, 30
spider monkey, 20
spider's web, 30
spinosaurus, 41
sponge, 10
spoonbill, 21
squirrel, 14, 31
squirrel's nest, 36
stable, 17
stallion (horse), 32
starfish, 6
starling, 31
stegosaurus, 41
stick insect, 25
stickleback, 5
stonefish, 10
stork, 36
storks' nest, 36
story book animals, 38
straw, 29
sunfish, 10
swallow, 4
swan, 4
swan (cob), 33
swan (cygnet), 33
swan (pen), 33
swarm of locusts, 37
swordfish, 11

tiger snake, 24
toad, 18
toadstool, 14
tom cat, 33
tongue, 34
tortoise, 28
toucan, 21
tractor, 17
tree, acacia, 13
tree, banana, 20
tree, baobab, 13
tree, cocoa, 20
tree, date palm, 18
tree, eucalyptus, 25
tree, gum, 25
tree, maple, 9
tree, oak, 15
triceratops, 41
tropical fish, 28
trough, 16
trunk (elephant's), 34
turkey, 17
turkey, wild, 9
turtle, 11
tusk, 34
tyrannosaurus rex, 41

W

wallaby, 25
walrus, 22
wart hog, 13
wasp, 31
wasps' nest, 31
water buffalo, 12
water lily, 4
water vole, 4
weasel, 14
weaver bird, 13
weaver birds' nest, 13
web, spider's, 30
webbed foot, 34
whale, 22
whale, school of, 37
whelk, 7
whippet, 27
whiskers, 35
wild turkey, 9
wing, 35
winged horse, 38
wolf, 8
wombat, 24
woodchuck, 9
woodcock, 15
woodpecker, 15
woolly mammoth, 40
woolly rhinoceros, 40
work horse, 17
worm, 14, 31
worm, silk, 28
wren, 5

u

unicorn, 38
urchin, sea, 6

t

tadpole, 4
tail, 34
talon, 35
tarantula, 18
Tasmanian wolf, 40
teeth, 35
termites' nest, 12
tern, 6, 23

V

vixen (fox), 33
vole, water, 4
vulture, 18

z

zebra, 12

47